CREATING A GOOD CUSTOMER SERVICE

How To Maintain A Good Buyer-Seller Relationship

Christopher P. Hill

All rights reserved. No part of this publication may be reproduced, distributed, or transmitted in any form or by any means, including photocopying, recording, or other electronic or mechanical methods, without the prior written permission of the publisher, except in the case of brief quotations embodied in critical reviews and certain other noncommercial uses permitted by copyright law.

Copyright © 2022 - Christopher P. Hill

TABLE OF CONTENTS

Chapter 1 4
Surviving In A Competitive Industry

Chapter 2 20
Customer Relationship Management (CRM)

Chapter 3 37
Service Strategy

Chapter 4 55
Do You Listen To Customers?

Chapter 1

Surviving In A Competitive Industry

Organizations have emphasized customer service more and more as a way to achieve a competitive edge throughout the years. Who would have thought, for instance, 15 years ago that companies like Amazon.com could take market share away from the high street by providing the client with a large range of affordable items supported by first-rate customer service? Or that businesses like First Direct might fundamentally alter how clients do business with their bank by providing a helpful, effective service around-the-clock, 365 days a year?

There is only one legitimate definition of a company objective, according to Peter Drucker, and that is to produce customers. According to him, an organization's capacity to stay in business depends on its ability to be competitive and to attract clients from other businesses. The customer is the cornerstone of the company and ensures its survival. Many businesses have come to the conclusion that they cannot compete on pricing alone as competition has gotten more global and fierce. Many businesses have created a strategy to distinguish their goods and services in these markets by offering outstanding customer service. According to surveys, service-driven businesses may charge up to 9% more for the goods and services they provide. They expand twice as quickly as the typical business and have the potential to capture up to 6% of the market.

The Royal Bank of Scotland turned a significant reform initiative meant to put the client first from being on the verge of a loss to generating an additional £200 million profit in only two years. Tesco, a retailer, became the market leader in a highly competitive and price-conscious sector by concentrating on the client and growing its profitability and market share. Financial services' shift in emphasis is typical of many industries toward providing for customers.

A growing emphasis is being placed on personal service as a way to add value for customers due to the nature and volume of competitors as well as the ability of retailers, banks, building societies, insurance brokers, estate agents, and other financial service companies to offer similar products at similar prices.

However, few businesses flourish in this market segment, just as in a lot of other ones taking the lead. Best-practice companies have shown that a customer-centric approach has demonstrable advantages in markets that are becoming more competitive.

A company that provides excellent service can:

- differentiate itself from the competition;
- improve its image in the eyes of the customer;
- minimize price sensitivity;
- improve profitability;
- increase customer satisfaction and retention;
- achieve a maximum number of advocates for the company;
- enhance its reputation;

- ensure products and services are delivered 'right first time';
- improve staff morale;
- increase employee satisfaction and retention;
- increase productivity;
- reduce costs;
- encourage employee participation;
- create a reputation for being a caring, customer-oriented company;
- foster internal customer/supplier relationships;
- bring about continuous improvements to the operation of the company.

There has been a lot of pressure on service firms in recent years to change how they interact with their clients. Poor service may also result in public humiliation, as the Passport Office discovered its expense when its Service Charter mark was revoked due to ineffective passport delays during the busy summer months. The challenge for a corporation today is to "inject" innovation into its core processes so that it becomes ingrained in every aspect of the firm. Higher standards of customer service are always sought by successful service businesses. When the online bookshop Amazon was founded, its creator realized it could not provide comfortable couches or coffee to individuals who browse through its virtual bookstore, so it went about finding creative methods to improve the consumer experience.

Few companies have been able to accomplish this effectively, but those that have are notable. When First Direct introduced a telephone banking service, it completely changed the retail banking industry. 38% of new customers came through referrals from current ones as a consequence of its emphasis on speed, convenience, quality, and service. Pret a Manger, a network of sandwich shops that began with one location in Victoria, currently has more than 500 locations.

The company attributes its success to a "connection of trust" with its consumers, meticulous attention to detail and ongoing innovation. In the last ten years, there has been a shift in organizational emphasis from product to customer. However, only a small number of businesses, such as online auction houses eBay, can be claimed to be really customer-centric: built around and motivated by clients.

Consumers in today's market are becoming smarter, educated, assured, and knowledgeable. They have high standards for the service they want to get. They don't want to be "sold to" or coerced, and they want more options. The 24-hour culture has already here. According to a Future Foundation analysis, more than 2 million individuals in the UK worked between 9 p.m. and 11 p.m. in 2007 and almost a million did so between 2 a.m. and 5 a.m.

Over 50% of respondents to a study that BT and First Direct jointly commissioned said they wanted public transportation and pharmacies open 24 hours a day. Additionally, a third of those polled want access to a variety of different retail establishments as well as sports, recreation, and entertainment facilities around the clock.

The 24-hour retail revolution is being led by supermarkets. In 1994, ASDA introduced the first 24-hour shops. In addition to offering home shopping from more than 100 locations, Tesco has 370 stores open 24/7 in 2007, up from 81 outlets in 1999. The home shopping service enables people to order goods online; the web page lists each customer's most frequently purchased items at the top of the list to aid selection; the order is then relayed to a computerized trolley, where on-board computers direct an order-picking assistant on the most practical path through the store to collect the groceries. Consumers are becoming more mobile and are seeking time-saving opportunities.

A third of small businesses and 40% of medium-sized businesses have personnel who are regularly mobile, according to research by MORI conducted for mobile phone providers Orange. They rely on technology to communicate with their office and the client. For instance, Veeder-Root is a business that creates, installs and maintains 8,000 devices that gauge the fuel levels in the underground tanks that are located under many of the UK's gas stations. So that they always have access to the most recent client information, field engineers are given wifi laptop computers. Prior to each visit, they may make a call to get the most recent customer survey and conduct on-site problem-solving without returning to the corporate headquarters. Productivity levels, as well as staff and customer satisfaction, have grown as a consequence of this procedure. Customers of today are more inclined to voice their concerns if they believe that their rights have been infringed because they are aware of their rights.

According to Henley Centre research, 35% of UK people think that they sometimes like complaining. Additionally, the study revealed that 42% of respondents had complained on the phone and 45% of adults had complained in person about receiving bad treatment. According to a MORI survey, the vast majority of consumers say social responsibility affects their decision to buy a product or use a service. Sales of a variety of companies, including Nike, Coca-Cola, and Shell, are in jeopardy due to consumer concern about environmental and human rights violations. Numerous consumer interest organizations have joined forces in the dispute over genetically modified food in an effort to halt its development.

A "pull" situation where the client is taking control is what is starting to emerge. This is made possible by new media, where online "infomediaries" (information intermediaries who find the best trading partner, make comparisons, and complete transactions) give consumers more options and websites have the opportunity to receive customer opinions that can be shared with a broad audience. According to a National Statistics poll, internet use is rising quickly in the UK, with more than half of the population having access to the internet at home or at work. The fax and the phone have been mostly replaced by email as a method of local and international communication due to their widespread use.

For many businesses, "mass marketing" their goods or services is no longer a profitable strategy. According to a DTI and CBI poll, creative, tailored goods and customer service are what really set marketing apart. Individualization and customization are crucial. bookstore online Because it is aware of a customer's past purchases, Amazon may provide customized service. You may personalize and distinguish a product at Levi's by visiting the store's personalized area. Organizations now have the opportunity to compete on a regional, national, and pan-continental level because of growing globalization. Using technology, Amazon.com has disrupted regional and international customer buying habits. Today's cyber rivals pose a danger to its market dominance. Nobody should savor their victories, is the message. Global rather than local competition exists.

The variety of options made possible by the expanding usage of technology is one of the biggest forces behind change. The use of technology has the potential to completely transform how businesses interact with their consumers, from online shopping for goods and services to utilize the internet to pay bills on a mobile device. Claims are processed immediately by Chubb Insurance Group; when representatives visit a client's location, they enter data using a laptop and immediately print a check. Peabody, a US home delivery shop, utilizes its client information to alert people when they are likely to run out of essentials for the home.

Cisco, a US-based maker of networking hardware, has given its customers the ability to self-serve via its website in real-time. Customers get immediate access to their online shopping information. According to the company, in a single year, this method of working saved Cisco $268 million, of which $125 million was saved on customer support (customers supported themselves online), $8 million was saved on recruitment and training (as this was moved online), $85 million was saved on software distribution costs (as the software was downloaded online), and $50 million was saved by switching to a paperless information distribution system. The usage of technology has grown, and with it the ability of the consumer to influence the future of consumer brands.

Today's web-enabled consumer has access to sites that allow for immediate pricing comparisons and user feedback. For instance, the website TripAdviser is a well-liked forum for travelers to publish their opinions and evaluations regarding resorts, hotels, and other leisure alternatives in the travel business. It has developed into a resource for discriminating travelers who place more value in the testimonials of other passengers than in the marketing campaigns of the service provider firms.

Corporations have realized as a result of the change in power that they can no longer promote and sell to customers the same way they once did. Today, a brand's success is jointly created by the business and its customers. Today, the consumer has a far greater say in the creation and success of goods and services. Just look at the popularity of websites like YouTube, the iPod, and Wikipedia. Dove, a consumer product from Unilever, has excelled in promoting women's self-worth and attractiveness. The need for businesses to engage their consumers in the creation and marketing of their goods and services seems to be increasing over time. Expectations raise when clients start receiving better services.

In the customer's opinion, the service received is also transportable. No matter the industrial sector, customers compare various service experiences on an instinctive and conscious level. Customers' expectations, for instance, of the customer service they will receive from a car rental service, may be based not only on their expectations and experiences of the service itself but also on experiences they may have had in-person or online, with other car rental companies and other leisure and travel organizations.

As a result, a company's capacity to draw in and keep new clients depends on more than just its product or product line. It also depends on how it treats its current clientele and on the reputation it builds in the local and global markets. However, a lot of businesses fail to see the potential that their current clientele has to help them grow. The majority of client bases for service businesses are made up of individuals who consume goods or services on a regular basis. At one extreme, certain clients would only ever do business with the company; at the other, clients could often utilize the goods or services of the firm. Customer loyalty programs have been overrun in recent years in sectors that are competitive.

The frequent flyer programs of the top airlines and the loyalty programs used by food merchants are some of the most well-known programs. In the UK, more than 150 loyalty programs have been formed over the last ten years, issuing more than 50 million cards at a cost of over £3 billion in incentives. Customer Loyalty Today estimates that 51% of British consumers have a loyalty card, and 70% of those who shop at supermarkets that provide them have one as well.

To provide the impression of developing a connection with clients, it appears like everyone is introducing loyalty programs, sending letters that are uniquely addressed, and creating tailored promos. But according to observable statistics and expected standards, only a small percentage of customers remain steadfast for a whole year, and those that usually only purchase a little quantity of the product or service. In fact, a lot of brands may compete for the allegiance of consumers. Customers will often purchase products and services from a range of options in a certain industry.

Because of this, customer loyalty programs may foster behavioral commitment but they may not ensure attitudinal loyalty if a rival business creates its own loyalty programs or the client redeems his or her rewards: they may still be just as vulnerable to varying goods or services as before. Furthermore, while not always in a favorable manner, incentive programs may alter consumers' perceptions of the product.

They could start to anticipate benefits on a regular basis, for instance. Companies investing in programs to improve customer loyalty may thus do so with confidence, knowing if the resultant changes in consumer behavior will result in higher profits from each client. Calculating the average yearly revenue and customer retention value results in a total revenue number from which costs may be subtracted to arrive at a gross profit, or lifetime value, for each customer.

Customer lifetime values have evolved into a pillar of ScotRail's new marketing approach, which has stopped the long-term fall in passenger volume. The business was able to measure the cause and effect link between service performance and retention rates using a new customer database and a lifetime framework model. This has thus made it possible for it to determine the expected changes to lifetime values in a variety of circumstances and adapt its customer service tactics as a result.

Chapter 2

Customer Relationship Management (CRM)

Customer relationship management (CRM) is a system that organizes all of your business's interactions and connections with current and future clients. The objective is straightforward: To expand your company, and improve business ties. Companies may enhance profitability, process efficiency, and client retention using a CRM system. When individuals mention CRM, they often mean a CRM system, a device that aids in contact management, sales management, agent productivity, and other tasks.

With the advent of CRM systems, it is now possible to maintain customer connections across the full customer lifecycle, including interactions with marketing, sales, digital commerce, and customer support. With the aid of a CRM solution, you can concentrate on the relationships that your business has with specific people, such as clients, service users, employees, or suppliers, over the course of the entire relationship. This includes attracting new clients, earning their business, and providing ongoing support and other services.

Everyone in the firm, whether in sales, customer service, business development, hiring, or marketing, now has a better approach to handling the external contacts and connections that are essential to success. With the help of a CRM solution, you can manage marketing campaigns, track service problems, track sales possibilities, and keep track of customer interactions all in one place. You can also make information about every customer interaction accessible to anybody at your business who may need it.

Data visibility and accessibility make it simpler to cooperate and boost productivity. Everyone working for your organization has access to information about customers' communications, purchases, most recent purchases, payments, and much more. A small firm, whose teams often need to discover ways to accomplish more with less, may benefit particularly from CRM since it can assist businesses of all sizes to accelerate business development. You can get a thorough picture of your clients using a CRM system. You can see everything in one location, including a straightforward dashboard that is customized and can inform you about a client's prior interactions with you, the progress of their purchases, any unresolved customer care concerns, and more.

You may also decide to incorporate details about their public social media activity, such as their preferences and dislikes and remarks they have made about you or your rivals. With a data-driven management strategy, marketers may utilize a CRM system to monitor and improve campaigns and leadership journeys. By better understanding the sales or prospect pipeline, forecasting is made easier and more precise.

Every chance or lead will be clearly visible to you, and a direct route from inquiry to sales will be shown. Moving beyond CRM as only a sales and marketing tool and integrating it into other aspects of your business, from finance to customer services and supply chain management, may result in some of the highest productivity benefits and a change in the whole organization toward customer-centricity.

This makes it easier to guarantee that business process and innovation cycles prioritize the demands of the client. Client care and support is a growing area of CRM and a crucial component in maintaining a comprehensive customer relationship, even though CRM systems have typically been utilized as tools for sales and marketing. The typical client of today may register a complaint on one platform, like Twitter, and then go to a private communication channel, like email or the phone, to address it.

By providing sales, support, and marketing with a single picture of the client to guide their actions, CRM software enables you to handle the inquiry across channels without losing track. For the purpose of providing personalized, integrated experiences, it is crucial to link these three tasks and the people who carry them out on a single platform. Less time for anything else due to increased administration. Data may be produced in plenty by a busy sales staff. While on the road, representatives speak with clients, meet prospects, and gather useful information, but all too often, this data is scribbled down in notebooks, kept on computers, or retained in the minds of your salespeople.

Details may be overlooked, meetings are not properly followed up on, and client prioritization is sometimes more of an art than a science based on facts. And if a key salesman leaves, it might all become worse. Without CRM, however, more than just sales suffer. You can get calls, emails, or messages on social media from consumers who have questions, want to follow up on purchases, or have a problem.

Without a standardized platform for client interactions, messages may be lost in the deluge of information or overlooked, which might result in a late or inadequate response. Even if you are successful in gathering all of this data, understanding it will be difficult. Intelligence gathering may be challenging. Reports may take a lot of work to produce and take up important selling time. A lack of supervision may also lead to a lack of responsibility from the team since managers might become blind to what their teams are doing and so are unable to provide the proper assistance at the appropriate moment.

By organizing customer and prospect information in a way that enables you to forge stronger relationships with them and expand your business more quickly, customer relationship management (CRM) solutions assist you in attracting new clients, securing their business, and maintaining their satisfaction. CRM systems begin by gathering data from a customer's website, email, phone, and social media accounts, among other sources and channels.

Additionally, it may automatically draw in other data, including current firm activity headlines, and it may keep private information, like a client's individual communication preferences. To help you fully comprehend your connection over time, the CRM application aggregates this data into a comprehensive record of people and organizations. A CRM system is then used to handle daily customer activities and interactions with a consolidated picture of every prospect and client. In terms of marketing, this entails engaging your prospects with the appropriate message at the appropriate moment using specialized digital marketing campaigns and journeys.

With a comprehensive perspective of their pipeline, sales representatives can anticipate more accurately and operate more efficiently. Business-to-consumer (B2C) and business-to-business (B2B) e-commerce teams can easily establish and expand from online orders to curbside pickup (B2B commerce). Additionally, customer care representatives may attend to client requirements on any channel from their homes, the field, or the office. Other business tools that support the development of customer connections may be linked to a CRM platform. Today's CRM systems are more flexible and link with your preferred business tools, like document signing, accounting and invoicing, and surveys, allowing information to flow both ways and providing you with a complete 360-degree perspective of your client.

However, the latest CRM generation goes one step further: Built-in intelligence and AI automate administrative duties, such as lead or service case routing and data input, so you have more time for worthwhile pursuits. Automatically produced insights assist you in better understanding your clients and even forecasting their feelings and behaviors so you can plan the appropriate outreach. AI may also assist you in uncovering opportunities that may be hiding in your company's data.

Many businesses are seeing their conventional markets and profit margins shrink due to the rising power of the consumer and the ferocious competition. Moving from a product orientation to a customer focus and ultimately a customer centricity is a problem facing the company today.

Being more customer-focused may be achieved by establishing a customer service infrastructure employing contact centers and web-enabled technologies. Currently, fundamental apps for contact centers get 75% of all technological investments. In a recent poll by KPMG Consulting, 89% of businesses said that they believe customer information to be crucial to the success of their company.

However, just 16% of those polled believed that their clients were making full use of the data they had supplied, and 12% couldn't estimate the number of clients they had. Organizations have the option to manage their connection with customers thanks to CRM systems. CRM operates on the premise that the more knowledge a business has about its clients, the better. Professor Adrian Payne of Cranfield University defines CRM as "the strategic process of identifying desirable customer segments, micro-segments, or individual customers on a one-to-one basis and developing integrated programs that maximize both values to the customer and the lifetime value of customers to the organization through targeted customer acquisition, profit-enhancing activities, and retention."

According to a KPMG survey, 43% of businesses were unable to pinpoint the major reasons behind disgruntled clients, and almost half were unable to pinpoint clients who were on the verge of leaving. As a company strategy, customer retention is increasingly becoming more important than searching for or acquiring new clients. According to Bain & Co. research, a 5% improvement in customer retention results in a 20–125% rise in net present value profits.

CRM refers to the management of the customer relationship across all of the customer's interactions with the business as a whole process. The "silo" attitude of conventional organizations is dismantled, and information about the client is shared, as opposed to treating customer interactions on an as-needed basis as, for example, a marketing contact or a request for customer assistance.

The fact that data has historically been kept in different portions of the firm is one of the issues that many companies face. Therefore, one department of a bank can be aware of a customer's current account status but not his or her mortgage status. From databases of current or future customers, a CRM system may aid in the identification of sales opportunities. It can support all facets of the sale, such as providing online access to order status and a unified view of the customer status once the transaction is complete.

It has the ability to gather data on the client and the inquiries that were made. In order to assist allocate resources, it may also be connected with pertinent databases and supply-chain management software, guaranteeing, for example, that the clients who generate the most revenue get the best quality of care. Additionally, it can track consumer use trends, allowing for the detection of irregularities or a drop in consumption. For instance, Capital One, a financial services company, uses "predictive service and selling." At crucial junctures in the life cycle, intelligent technology urges an agent to get in touch with the consumer. The key to a successful CRM is customer insight and expertise.

However, organizations won't be able to satisfy customers whose wants are continually changing if this information isn't shared and used across the firm. Implementing a CRM strategy entails connecting systems from sales, marketing, IT, customer support, and finance in order to centralize information. Because of cultural barriers including internal departments' reluctance to share information, it might fail with a high failure rate. According to CRM data from Accenture Consulting, a typical US $1 billion firm would realize US $40 million more in earnings with a 10% improvement in CRM capabilities.

All of a customer's interactions with a firm contribute to how they view the quality of the service. A company must thus strengthen all facets of its interaction with clients in order to improve the quality of its services. Customers often don't see an organization's service as a whole when they use it. Customers' opinions of an organization are shaped by the little details of their interactions with them, such as a letter that was sent to the wrong address, a significant wait in obtaining an email answer, or a service that wasn't as described. The experiences of businesses that have implemented programs to enhance service quality inside their organizations provide lessons that may be used.

Many companies have focused their efforts on staff employees who interact with customers directly in an attempt to increase quality. They fail to include support, headquarters, and other staff members in a cycle of quality improvement. It's like healing a head trauma after the poison has already spread to the rest of the body via the bloodstream to enhance customer service at the frontline level inside a corporation.

A service firm has no barriers, according to research. It is a transparent factory, in other words, for the client. Customers hold the whole business accountable for low standards, not specific employees. The management is ultimately responsible for making sure that a system is in place to handle bookings efficiently and effectively, that staff members have been properly trained, and that good lines of communication exist between all parts of the organization and the customer in the event that a customer arrives at a hotel for a pre-arranged booking only to find that he or she has no room for the night.

Many firms learn that a program to strengthen team members' abilities in order to improve service quality from the bottom up falls short since it does not change the company's management ingrained views. Because managers seem to say one thing while doing another and because fundamental issues that are present across the company are not addressed, team members may respond to such projects with skepticism.

It's critical to keep in mind that every employee of a firm performs a service while discussing consumers. There are "external" and "internal" customers. Internal customers are undervalued in far too many firms. To deliver a good or service to a customer on time and according to their specifications, a long chain of people may be needed, including those involved in product development, purchasing, manufacturing, warehousing, and delivery. Each person in this chain must also consider the needs of their subordinates. Suppliers and customers are their internal relationships.

If the client wants to obtain outstanding service, done correctly the first time, it is extremely essential to treat everyone with respect, provide work that is free of errors, and so on. The standard of "silent service"—the support that employees provide to one another—often determines the quality of the service that is delivered to the client. If workers don't feel their employer values them, they won't care about their customers.

Managers should not see the individuals who report to them as workers but rather as clients for whom they have a duty to provide first-rate service. If the company's internal service provider has in turn gotten top-notch service from his or her internal supplier, the likelihood that the external client will obtain a decent service increases significantly. Customers' perceptions of a company's corporate social responsibility and how far enterprises go to uphold ethical standards are increasingly influencing how involved they are with the brand. The influence an organization has on the economy, society, environment, and human rights is something that consumers now take into consideration.

Customers are increasingly scrutinizing an organization's ethical ideals and the impact it makes outside of its local business environment in the wake of corporate crises like the Enron crisis in the United States. Many companies today strive to "give back" to society by making a contribution that benefits the larger community or environment. Effective corporate social responsibility initiatives may also result in financial gains. In a recent study conducted at the University of Chicago by Professor Curtis Verschoor and published in Management Accounting in February 2006, it was discovered that businesses with a clearly stated corporate commitment to ethical principles outperform businesses without such a commitment financially. Nike's profits fell by 27% as a result of the public outcry over its slave labor practices and slave pay for foreign labor. Customers are also growing more conscious of environmental problems. By 2008, Wal-Mart hopes to sell 100 million ecologically friendly lightbulbs, saving $3 billion in power. Tesco is "carbon-labelling" its 70,000 items. And GE is investing US $1.5 billion annually in a program dubbed Ecomagination that seeks to promote green technology.

Chapter 3

Service Strategy

Here, we'll look at how to develop an organizational culture that puts the needs of the customer first and bases company operations on a customer service strategy. It offers helpful examples and guidance on how business executives may show their dedication to providing excellent customer service while also launching and directing a service improvement initiative within their company.

According to an Institute of Management analysis, the primary obstacles to firms obtaining greater levels of customer care are seen to be a concentration on short-term objectives, a lack of commitment from senior management, and a lack of training. Evidence suggests that senior management's engagement in terms of time, money, effort, dedication, tenacity, and visibility is necessary for service excellence to be seen as a crucial success element in a company's long-term survival. A clear message emerges from Unisys research on how more than 80 firms across the globe have effectively ingrained excellent customer service into their corporate cultures.

The study shows that the best-practice firms are those whose service improvement activities are led, directed, and guided from the top. Leaders in the industry don't just pay lip service to the idea; they invest real money and put in a lot of work to establish customer-driven organizations. George Cox, the former CEO of Unisys UK, emphasized that pronouncements from above are useless unless they are followed by deeds: "No CEO is going to declare his firm ignores the customer." To permeate the whole firm with the mindset that the client actually counts, though, the top person needs to believe it.

The difficulty, according to Levi Strauss Chairman Bob Hass, is to combine "the soft stuff of worker empowerment with the hard stuff of getting jeans through the door." The pursuit of service excellence never ends. Over the last ten years, businesses like Scandinavian Airlines have been engaged in a continuous campaign to enhance the level of service they provide to their consumers.

The dedication and vision of the organization's executives to a service philosophy and the creation of a service strategy meant to support this philosophy underpin this program, as well as many others of best-practice companies. Each of them is aware that changing the culture may take up to five years in order to bring about service quality improvements.

Managing And Leading

Managers often keep things moving. To accomplish their goals, they establish processes, monitor their progress, and set goals. Change is facilitated more by leaders. They emphasize motivating others, developing long-term plans, providing examples for others to follow, and coaching for improved performance. One of the most important distinctions between managers and leaders is that while managers concentrate on the now, leaders concentrate on the future and search for new approaches. Leaders use a proactive strategy rather than a reactive one. Experience has taught us that managers must also exhibit leadership traits in order to foster a culture of excellent customer service.

To provide top-notch service, they must inspire and drive their employees. Importantly, they must serve as examples of the company values and behaviors that support good customer service. Because of this, it's crucial that managers from every department participate in the process right away when a firm starts a service excellence program. The health company BUPA put all of its managers through service leadership training as part of a drive to enhance the quality of its customer service.

This was done to assist them to serve as role models for service excellence. During this phase, managers underwent a 360-degree feedback process to determine their leadership strengths and potential growth areas. The program's overall impact meant that management personnel was better prepared to drive the necessary changes before their team members attended their portion of the service excellence program.

Professors Kotter and Heskett of the Harvard Business School contend that a company's capacity for change is directly related to its leadership style. It is necessary for the workforce as a whole to realize that unless changes are made, the firm will lose consumers in order to promote a focus on the customer. Business executives should also express the need for change and set an example for others to follow. The former CEO of GEC, Jack Welch, focused his efforts on transforming his company's culture such that important values guided business decisions.

These principles include agility, candor (including constructive conflict), ownership, quickness (in execution), simplicity (in idea and communication), and self-confidence (via delegating and empowerment) (from a flexible and lean organization). Leadership has changed from the traditional command and control method to a new enabling approach that attempts to unleash the potential of the workforce in today's more responsive environment. A lot has been written on leadership, leadership styles, and the traits of effective leaders. The situational and the visionary camps have traditionally made up the majority of leadership ideologies.

According to situational leadership theory, leaders evaluate a situation and take appropriate action. Their actions depend on the circumstances around them. The level of expertise or knowledge possessed by their teams and the degree to which they need emotional support are the two main concerns that effective leaders would pay special attention to.

Tailoring Your Vision To Serve The Customer

Establishing a mindset with customer service at its center is the first step on the path to excellence. This philosophy may be outlined in terms of the organization's mission statement, which outlines its goals and objectives, or its vision statement, which outlines the company's core principles. The phrases "mission" and "vision" are sometimes ambiguous. Whatever the nomenclature, a mission or vision should capture what the staff accepts and believes to be the fundamental values that set the tone for how they should conduct themselves at work. Upon taking over as ICI's chairman, John Harvey-Jones set out to give the business a new sense of purpose via a series of deeds that had both a practical and symbolic impact.

He changed the location of the ICI board of directors meetings from the intimidating and formal board room at Millbank to his office. The directors were seated in plush chairs with side tables connected for their notes while wearing shirt sleeves. This modification made it easier for everyone to work together and participate in the decision-making process. The rest of the company received a strong message that a new set of values was being developed, which was far more potent than any amount of words could have been.

According to surveys, 90% of big companies have created a mission statement in the previous five years, making it the most often used management tool.

There are compelling arguments for developing one as the average return on shareholder equity for companies with mission statements is 16.1%, compared to 9.7% for those without. A mission statement is often beneficial, but creating a visionary firm requires many other actions as well. The management expert Peter Drucker asserts: "Determining what business an organization is in is one of the most significant things an organization can accomplish." A vision is a torch-bearer for an organization's mission.

It provides a response to the query, "What are we here for?" It offers a glimpse of a different and better future than the one we now live in. A shared understanding of the direction the company is taking should result from the development of a vision. It has to be ambitious and motivating. It ought to encourage workers to forge a shared goal.

Different companies use a variety of strategies to establish their visions. Generally speaking, the vision is little more than a paragraph and is stated in plain terms. Before creating a common vision, best-practice businesses engage with all parties, including workers. Everyone will know what they are working for and what is expected of them in order to contribute to the success of the business.

For instance, Morgan Stanley, a financial services company, has the goal of becoming "one firm corporation." The biggest fish and chip shop in the world, according to The Guinness Book of Records, is Harry Ramsden's. The firm had a great reputation, but John Barnes, the Chairman of Harry Ramsden's plc, realized it had lost its course when he purchased it.

His plan for the company called for restoring the principles that had made it so successful in the past and then expanding on them to secure an even better future. In order to learn about the finest practices that were carried out while "Old Harry" was around, John Barnes spent his first few months in the company getting to know staff groups. To find out what the customers thought of the company, he established customer groups. He developed an overarching vision for the company with the management group on the basis of this study. NASA was a very inconspicuous organization until President Kennedy's ambition of "a man on the moon in the 1960s" elevated it to a valuable national asset. This grand goal inspired not just the personnel of NASA but also the thousands of helpers who worked for NASA and the whole country. The dedication was made to the vision rather than to Kennedy. The realization of the vision after his passing is evidence of its uniting aspect.

An organization, department, or business unit must take a step back and consider its goals before developing a vision. It must concentrate on the core components that both characterize it and determine success or failure. Senior management inside the business must take ownership of and be committed to the vision. A specifically called gathering is often when a vision is agreed upon.

When this is overseen by an unbiased facilitator who is not a member of the management team, it might sometimes be beneficial.

The meeting's goal is to reach an agreement among the team members on a vision statement. The vision must not contain anything to which top management is not committed, since failing to do so would render it useless. It should also be written in a language that is accessible to everyone. Asking coworkers, clients, consumers, workers, shareholders, and rivals the following questions might be a helpful place to start when developing a vision:

- What do we want this organization to be and to stand for?
- Where and how we are going to delight our customers?
- What do we want people in this organization to be good at?
- How do we want them to behave?
- What do we have to be good at to succeed in this market or industry?

According to an EC-funded study on HR development, most chief executives struggle to communicate the company's mission to different employee groups. The majority of those questioned workers were unaware of the organization's vision or goal. There is often a risk that they may be seen by workers of a firm as meaningless platitudes. However, if workers are engaged in the vision's formulation, this risk may be avoided.

One computer corporation, for instance, collaborated with its management team to create a vision statement before distributing it across the whole organization. Senior managers had one-on-one conversations about the vision with each of their managers, who then had these conversations with their workers. The manager and the employee signed a short booklet that was created to help with the conversation and it was given to them as a reminder.

At the conclusion of the meeting, the manager provided top management with a summary of the conversations she had with each employee, along with recommendations for improving the vision. Customers are involved in the vision formulation process at other businesses. NatWest Life was able to start on a blank slate because of thorough consumer attitude research. According to the study, companies needed to prioritize customer satisfaction as their main responsibility if they were to succeed in developing lasting connections with their clients. Their mission statement said, "Our clients are the center of all we do. We cherish our customers and will give great service and listen to their input." This captures this.

Normally once a year, missions and visions should be reviewed to make sure they still fit with the organization's internal and external environment. Since Tom Farmer launched the tire and exhaust repair business Kwik-Fit in 1971, dedication to clients has been a top emphasis. Its goal was to provide "100% pleasure, 100% of the time." Since then, Kwik-Fit has capabilities for consumers to record their issues or recommendations and to stay in touch with them. Receipts are accompanied by customer surveys, and a dedicated, free phone service is available 24/7. Every suggestion is appreciated, and action is taken.

Senior management must be clear on the organization's values if they are to turn the vision into reality. In this sense, "values" refers to those widely held presumptions and ideas that really have an impact on how individuals behave. What matters to the way the company runs, in other words. The founder William Mayo's maxim, "The best interest of the patient is the sole interest to be considered," influences choices at the US Mayo Clinic on a daily basis. Care is arranged on patient requirements rather than physicians' schedules, hospital procedures, or any other aspect relating to Mayo Clinic's internal operations, as shown by solid and consistent evidence.

The sense of pride and the alignment of employee attitudes with Mayo's principles help to reduce staff turnover, which is 4 percent for nurses compared to the industry average of 20 percent. A deeply held value may be reflected in the vision itself. For instance, the Body Shop's mission is unmistakably impacted by the importance of employing only natural, non-animal-tested goods. The process used to produce the vision reflects corporate values as well. Is it, for instance, the work of a small number of top managers, or has the notion of involvement and listening to colleagues already been ingrained in the corporate culture? Values are frequently referred to as "the cultural glue" of a company.

Every company has a unique culture. The way people dress, keep their surroundings clean, and behave are all examples of culture. Other aspects include the language spoken, how hospitable people are, and how well they listen. These have the organization's shared ideals at their core. What, for instance, are the actual priorities: customer service, cost reduction, or adhering to what the business requires? Culture matters because it influences how much innovation and energy individuals bring to their jobs and because it may win or lose clients. NFC is one business that appreciates the impact corporate values may have on its ability to generate profits (The National Freight Corporation).

The business maintained strong levels of success throughout the 1990s. The culture of employee share ownership and the excitement it has fostered in the business are what the organization refers to as its "hidden plus factor" and play a significant role in its success. Senior management's dedication to and conviction in the organization's basic principles enhances this. Employee ownership, quality, internationalism, people development, social responsibility, and premium performance are the values listed by NFC.

According to surveys, up to 90% of managers anticipate that values will become even more crucial for organizational performance over the next three years, with 85% of those surveyed believing that "the team needs the stability and direction of distinct corporate values" during times of rapid change. There is evidence that an organization's ability to predict and respond to changes in the business environment relies on having values that support this. Egg, a provider of online financial services, has created a set of principles that guide its company behavior. Senior leadership saw the critical need for a cultural transformation at the time First Quench was established as a joint venture between Allied Domecq and Whitbread. The purpose, vision, and values were developed over the course of two board meetings.

The company's purpose and values were then established via a team activity that a trial group of 60 head office employees participated in to guarantee that people would support change. The Alchemy transformation software was then made available to all staff. To ensure that the principles were ingrained in every aspect of the firm, reminders, workbooks, cassettes, and other materials were circulated across the organization.

The organization's enduring purpose (mission), which is to "Process the power of information to offer people all the help they need," and its strategic intent (vision) for the next three years, which is to "create a stunning and individual experience for customers and employees while driving extended value for shareholders," was introduced in conjunction with the values. Early on in the merger, the two firms that made up the insurance company CGU realized they had differing corporate principles. They organized a number of workshops with the goal of developing a new set of core principles that put the interests of employees, business intermediates, and consumers at the forefront. However, Kevin Newman, the former CEO of First Direct, issues a word of caution: "Values will achieve absolutely nothing if people don't believe them. People will lose direction if ideals and practice are at odds, but when it works, it may have significant positive effects.

Chapter 4

Do You Listen To Customers?

Getting input from consumers is a crucial initial step in the creation of any service initiative. If businesses want to both bring in new consumers and keep their current ones, they must listen to their customers. Market research is a crucial component of creating a customer care program and a very effective tool for tracking the development of customer service efforts. Many businesses do not include concrete metrics in their customer care programs to assess how well service excellence enhancements are working.

Here, we'll talk about how you gauge both internal and external customer satisfaction by talking to consumers. According to a recent poll, 86% of business leaders identify as customer-centric. However, often times when people enter the workplace they cease being customers. Ritz Carlton is an exception. All Ritz Carlton staff members have received training in reading clients' emotions and identifying their preferences. These choices are included in a database of guest histories that contains preferences for 250,000 visitors. Staff members are better equipped to comprehend clients and foresee and manage their expectations as a result. Organizations often assume they understand the needs of their clients, yet this assumption may be based on a subjective rather than an objective perspective. The following are some of the obstacles that stop businesses from being close to their clients:

- The evidence of anecdotal events which occur on a one-off basis and can cloud a manager's opinion;

- The views of complainants which are often not counterbalanced by non-complainants; a high percentage of customers do not complain only one in 26 people is the figure often quoted, based on research undertaken in the United States;

- The opinions of a strongly articulate group of customers which may

- Cloud an organization's view of customer requirements;

- Preconceptions within the organization – the 'we have always done.

- It this way and this is what the customer wants' syndrome.

All of these things impede businesses from really knowing how effectively their goods and services meet consumer expectations. Compiling a cost diary and estimating the professional and personal expenses of each error that happens, as well as the savings that might have been realized based on avoidance, is a valuable way to assess the cost of mistakes that go unnoticed.

Best-practices organizations aggressively welcome complaints. One of the telltale symptoms of a poor or deteriorating relationship with a client is the lack of complaints, according to business expert Theodore Levitt. Nobody ever feels so content, certainly not for a long time. Either the client is not being truthful or they are not being contacted. The assessment of complaints and compliments is sometimes inaccurate since, on average, a tiny portion of a company's client base actually bothers to complain, and fewer individuals bother to thank a company. Furthermore, interactions with front-line employees often shape how consumers see a company.

Customers see these employees as representing the company, therefore any concerns they have are often focused at this level. It usually takes a significant occurrence for a complaint to get beyond the level of front-line employees. As a result, top management may not have much direct interaction with consumers, making it difficult for them to really comprehend their issues. Organizations sometimes get complaints, but they are only the tip of the iceberg. However, research indicates that consumers tell 10 other individuals about each negative service experience. With the advent of more internet use, these numbers are certain to soar. However, it is crucial that businesses offer the minority of consumers who do contact them personally the respect they deserve by implementing a successful procedure for handling both praises and complaints.

Customers are actually more inclined to complain if they want to keep their connection with the service provider, according to research by MORI. Therefore, encouraging a readiness to listen to criticisms is definitely worth doing. Camden Council often distributes promotional materials regarding its complaint mechanism and has advertised in the neighborhood press. A dissatisfied client is giving the business another chance to make things right and will be fair if handled honestly.

A customer's complement gives a company the chance to acknowledge the service provider's efforts and to use the compliment as an example of best practices. Analyzing complaints and praises in terms of their source, nature of the complaint or compliment, and frequency of occurrence is helpful.

It is also helpful to keep note of how long it takes to acknowledge a complaint; a prompt reply or, preferable, a phone call to do so is crucial, as is how long it takes to remedy the problem. The car rental corporation Avis has looked into potential acquisitions. It found that 92% of consumers who had no concerns would make another purchase from it. 91% of customers who had a problem, complained, and were satisfied were likely to make another purchase.

Customers who had a problem but didn't report it saw a decline in repurchase intention to 78%. Only 46% of consumers who had a problem, complained, and weren't happy, nevertheless, said they would buy from the business again. A customer care balance sheet is a helpful tool to better analyze the effect of complaints.

It reveals to the company how much revenue it is losing from both non-complaining consumers and those who do complain but are dissatisfied with the resolution of their issue. Periodically, postal surveys may be used to question both happy and dissatisfied customers about their experiences, as well as how many people they will tell if they are dissatisfied and if they plan to utilize the company's services again as a consequence.

The first factor is revenue lost from consumers who had a problem and complained but were dissatisfied with how their issue or inquiry was handled. (Sales lost consist of sales from consumers who won't use the service again and sales lost through unfavorable word-of-mouth marketing.) The second factor is revenue lost from clients who encountered a problem but did not file a complaint. Once again, the lost sales come from both consumers who won't use the service again and sales lost through unfavorable word-of-mouth marketing.

Sales that would have been lost due to regular attrition are subtracted from these two components. As opposed to only relying on complaints research, listening to consumers and actively seeking out input leads to improvements in service quality. For instance, the British Airports Authority (BAA) conducts over 120,000 consumer interviews each year. They are asked to rate several facets of the service they get. BAA utilizes the study to gauge how satisfied consumers are with the changes.

For instance, BAA asserts that the implementation of retail regulations has improved its value-for-money ratings at Heathrow. The corporation conducted in-depth consumer research after creating its value guarantee campaign at Heathrow and Gatwick to make sure that customers' opinions of airport shopping in terms of fairness and value for money fulfilled expectations. To meet their expectations, the vacation firm Butlins has worked hard to get to know its clients on a personal level.

Only a third of seasonal employees had any customer service training, only 5% thought their boss was engaged in handling complaints, and only 1% of reservations were complaints, according to a poll of seasonal employees. The business has employed market research to carry out targeted, unbiased studies on customer satisfaction and the sort of product customers desire from it. The foundation of a product, which is updated yearly depending on client feedback, stems from such a study. Since its founding over 60 years ago, Butlins is currently attaining the greatest level of consumer satisfaction, according to NOP research.

Customers are visiting its centers in record numbers, and the number of complaints has fallen too far below 0.3% of reservations. Information technology is used to analyze research, spot patterns, gauge repeat business, record client complaints, and follow their resolution. Therefore, effective service quality programs start by talking to consumers. Before launching a service effort, it's critical to get client feedback on the level of service that a company offers.

It is crucial that customer satisfaction metrics be based on their opinions of what matters rather than those held by the company. Prior to the launch of a service improvement program, customer surveys may be conducted to offer a baseline for tracking the success of a service campaign. It's not necessary to limit consumer listening to people outside the company. NatWest Life measures customer satisfaction ratings among the second group of consumers, the parent bank's specialized sales staff of personal financial advisors, in addition to conducting routine surveys of policyholders.

The results of the first study offered an astonishing bar for the quality of service offered by the 12 main life offices. According to this poll, 64% of the sales force was happy with the service these offices offered. In its first year of operation, the firm established a preliminary goal of achieving at least 70% adviser satisfaction. By the conclusion of the first year, 76% of sellers said they were "very happy" or thought NatWest Life's service was "outstanding".

The sales force's feedback has been so encouraging that NatWest Life has decided to cease combining the "excellent" and "very happy" rating categories and instead concentrate on "excellent" as an objective. The internet is being utilized more often to get client feedback. The challenge with online surveys is that they are often seen as spam, therefore the more personalized, intriguing, and engaging the email, the greater the response rate. The consumer is often provided with a link to the survey through email, such as "Click here to answer."

The best practice is to additionally provide a real-time notice if help is required to complete the survey. The business may then contact the client via phone or email to provide support. Online surveys have the advantage of offering continuous, real-time information, which is their main advantage. This implies that the results are updated as soon as a consumer provides their answer. After the consumer completes the survey, many businesses provide them rapid access to the data to guarantee a high response rate. Other businesses utilize their websites to solicit immediate client feedback. If management is not dedicated to the process and is unlikely to act on the findings, monitoring customer happiness is useless.

Therefore, before a program starts, it is important to explicitly outline the monitoring goals along with a budget and schedule. Managers must first choose the aspects of customer satisfaction to measure. Customers vary in their expectations, which affects how satisfied they are with the services received from a company. Market segments are groupings of consumers whose wants, expectations, and levels of satisfaction may differ significantly and who should be included in any study. Consider the various requirements of an airline's business and leisure passengers, for instance.

Before doing the study and performing the analysis, the sampling technique must be chosen. When creating a measuring strategy, it's common to overlook the presentation of outcomes. Results won't be taken into consideration unless they are presented in a way that the report's readers can easily handle and comprehend. The report's goal should be to empower managers and employees to act on the results of the surveys. If research findings are not rapidly communicated to the company, they lose all relevance. For instance, customer satisfaction scores at Domino's Pizza locations in America are made available to the public 24 hours after the research is finished.

Porsche UK is a leader in the "instant response" feedback method, which allows dealerships to receive client feedback immediately by email, letter, or phone. Customers of each firm will have unique service needs that must be evaluated. The customer's opinion of importance should be used to measure service standards, not the organization's. It is crucial that these areas are likewise seen as crucial in the perspective of consumers since many businesses focus their measurement on what they perceive to be the "risk spots" in terms of customer service.

The idea of customer connections has drawn the attention of many progressive organizations. This interest came about very organically as a result of marketing-focused firms' exploration of the advantages of client retention. Numerous studies (e.g., Heskett et al., 1994; Jones & Sasser, 1995; Reichheld & Sasser, 1990) have focused on this relatively new orientation toward customer retention, and it has led many businesses to change their previous sales orientation in favor of developing "relationships" with their clients; to reorient themselves toward retaining, as well as attracting, clients; to design and develop products and services that are better targeted to meet the needs of specific clients

Unfortunately, without a clear knowledge of what a relationship really is or if a client wants to build one, many businesses have jumped right into the creation of customer connections. As a consequence, almost every campaign that is widely designed to enhance consumer patronage is referred to as "relationship marketing" inside many marketing firms. Companies from a wide range of sectors have introduced a wide range of strategies to increase client loyalty and customize marketing campaigns to particular consumers. These typically consist of loyalty programs, direct marketing using databases, frequency marketing, and, more recently, relationship-building initiatives.

The fact that many strategies and initiatives put in place under the guise of relationship marketing have little to no actual relationship-building with clients is a serious flaw in their design. In reality, there is evidence that some efforts to forge "relationships" with consumers have instead alienated them by using methods that they dislike and see as "pushy" or invasive (Fournier, Dobscha & Mick 1998). Such programs go against some of the fundamental principles governing the development of relationships. According to focus group studies, most service providers with whom clients contact do not refer to their interactions as "relationships."

This isn't meant to imply that there aren't any real connections between companies and their clients, only that most of such encounters won't be referred to as relationships by clients. Such language is only used in "exceptional" situations. There are close client relationships, and they flourish when the consumer has a sincere feeling of commitment to the service provider. Several articles have been published on relationships in marketing, and numerous initiatives that have been launched under the banner of relationship marketing obviously have nothing to do with creating or maintaining relationships that meet the needs of the client *(Barnes 1994; 1995a)*.

In reality, many of the contacts that consumers have with companies and other organizations are one-off transactions that have little chance of developing into something that would be worthy of the term relationship. Even a string of frequent and regular encounters over a lengthy period of time could not be seen as a relationship by the client.